C000220483

A Year In My
Fenland Kitchen

A Year In My
Fenland Kitchen

by Annie Graves

Published in Great Britain in 2022 by Eyrie Press
www.eyriepress.co.uk

ISBN 978-1-913149-26-0

All rights reserved. No part of this book may be reproduced,
stored in a retrieval system, or transmitted in any form, or by any
means, electronic, mechanical, photocopying, recording or otherwise,
without prior written permission from the publisher.

All photographs © Annie Graves

A catalogue record of this book is available
from the British Library.

For Rob, Hannah and Abigail

ABOUT THE AUTHOR

I am a lifelong, enthusiastic collector of recipes and cookbooks.

Aged eight, I was that child who looked on the back of packets of Stork margarine and wrote off for the free recipe books and who, at the breakfast table, checked the boxes of cereal for ideas and recipes. I was the student who went off to university armed not only with clothes and books, but an array of baking equipment too.

In my early twenties, I read and re-read Delia Smith's *Complete Cookery Course*. Nowadays, I have shelves full of cookery books and, more often than not, can be found with my head in a book by Nigel Slater or Diana Henry.

So when Jane from Eyrie Press approached me with the idea of writing a cookbook of my own, it was a dream come true!

THANKS

I owe a huge debt of gratitude to Jane for all her hard work in helping to bring my dream of a book to fruition. And to my husband Rob, aka Mr Digandweed, for a lifetime of love and support, for being the muscle-power behind the allotment, and for making endless cups of tea.

CONTENTS

Spring

Summer

Autumn

Winter

INTRODUCTION

More than a decade ago now, my husband, Rob (aka Mr Digandweed) and I took on an allotment on the edge of the small Fenland market town where we live.

In the intervening years, we have tended this little patch of ground, and in return it has given us plentiful supplies of fresh veg and fruit.

About the same time as acquiring the allotment, I started writing a blog, *Fenland Lottie*, as a means of recording what we grew, the successes and the failures, and the meals that I made with our produce. As a result, along with my love of growing and cooking, I developed a love of photography.

This book has grown out of that blog. The recipes, whilst not strictly vegetarian, are mostly plant-based, often using the vegetables and fruit from the allotment and following the seasons as they unfold.

I have really enjoyed the process of developing, testing and photographing the recipes for the book and hope, equally, that you will enjoy reading and trying some of them for yourself.

Annie

A LOVE LETTER TO THE FENS

The Fens haven't always been my home.

I arrived here one cold and snowbound January day, more years ago than I care to remember, to take up my first job as a teacher in a local primary school. I stayed and slowly put down roots in these flat lowlands.

Moving from the rolling hills of the West Country, it took me a while to become accustomed to the Fens, criss-crossed by dykes and ditches and rivers, where the uninterrupted views are endless and the horizon disappears from sight. Their beauty is not immediately obvious. No mountains, lakes or waterfalls at which to gasp, instead a sense of space, solitude and peace. Summer days with a huge, blue sky canopy above fields of golden corn; autumn days, when the ploughed fields stretch out unencumbered by hedge or wood, the rich, brown soil like crumbled chocolate; winter with leaden skies and a row of trees in the far distance, like sentinels, just visible in the mist; and spring, when the banks of the lodes burst into life with the green shoots of reeds, and a swan swims serenely, followed by her brood of fluffy, grey cygnets.

These are the reasons I grew to love the Fens.

Probably more than any other region of Britain, the Fens have been moulded by the hand of man. They have a fascinating history.

Also known as the Fenlands, they cover a region in eastern England extending over parts of Lincolnshire, Cambridgeshire and Norfolk. Many centuries ago, they comprised a huge area of marsh and wet woodland, connected by shifting channels of water and the occasional island of higher ground. Some attempts to tame this wild and inaccessible landscape had already been made, but it wasn't until the seventeenth century that this began in earnest, when the 4th Earl of Bedford employed a Dutch engineer named Cornelius Vermuyden to systematically drain the land, a plan which was met with fierce opposition from local people who relied on the rich wildfowl and fish populations for their livelihoods.

Unfortunately, drainage caused not only the loss of large amounts of the 'black gold' peat due to shrinkage, but also the destruction of many rare species of flora and fauna. But now there are exciting, extensive and long-term plans, such as the Great Fen project, which aim to restore large areas to the original fen landscape, thereby safeguarding the future of many endangered species as well as mitigating the effects of climate change.

The story of the Fens has come full circle.

For more information on the history of the Fens, see www.greatfen.org.uk

CONVERSION TABLES

The recipes in this book use metric measurements. If you'd rather use imperial, these conversion tables may be helpful.

LIQUID CONVERSIONS

Metric	Imperial
60ml	2fl oz
75ml	2½fl oz
100ml	3½fl oz
150ml	5fl oz
200ml	7fl oz
300ml	10fl oz
400ml	13fl oz
500ml	17fl oz
600ml	20fl oz
700ml	24fl oz
800ml	28fl oz
900ml	32fl oz
1 litre	34fl oz

WEIGHT CONVERSIONS

Metric	Imperial
50g	2oz
75g	2½oz
100g	3½oz
125g	4oz
150g	5oz
175g	6oz
200g	7oz
225g	8oz
250g	9oz
300g	10½oz
350g	12oz
400g	14oz
450g	1lb

LINEAR CONVERSIONS

Metric	Imperial
2-3mm	⅛in
5mm	¼in
1cm	½in
2.5cm	1in
4cm	1½in
6cm	2½in
10cm	4in
15cm	6in
18cm	7in
20cm	8in
23cm	9in
25cm	10in
30cm	12in

OVEN TEMPERATURE CONVERSIONS

°C (fan)	°F (fan equivalent)	°C (non-fan)	Gas
90°C	190°F	110°C	gas ¼
100°C	210°F	120°C	gas ½
120°C	250°F	140°C	gas 1
130°C	265°F	150°C	gas 2
140°C	280°F	160°C	gas 3
160°C	320°F	180°C	gas 4
170°C	340°F	190°C	gas 5
180°C	350°F	200°C	gas 6
190°C	375°F	220°C	gas 7
200°C	400°F	230°C	gas 8
220°C	425°F	240°C	gas 9

Spring

Spring, and just lately the birds have been gathering in the trees outside the window, welcoming the new day and the changing season with their joyous song. And, in the garden, the tiny bobbing heads of the miniature narcissi are just opening. There is change in the air!

Spring is a busy time on the allotment. We have barrowloads of homemade compost to spread on the growing beds. All the scraps of kitchen waste, cardboard packaging and grass cuttings, carefully collected and mixed over the months, have resulted in a rich, brown mulch full of veggie-growing goodness. Plans have been made, seeds have been sorted; we are ready to start on a new growing season.

One of the first things to be planted each year are a few new potatoes. For some weeks now, the wizened tubers have been sitting on the windowsill of the spare room, propped up drunkenly in old egg boxes whilst they grow stubby little shoots, rather like spiky whiskers. In a week or two, we will dig a deep trench, pop the tubers at the bottom, cover them with soil and wait for our harvest of freshly dug potatoes to be ready in early summer.

SMOKED HADDOCK CHOWDER

If you have a few potatoes, new or otherwise, in the kitchen cupboard and some smoked haddock in the fridge, this recipe is perfect for a spring day, when you still want something warm and filling for supper.

INGREDIENTS

Serves 2–3

1 medium leek
a knob of butter
180g potatoes
300ml milk
100ml vegetable stock
a pinch of chilli flakes
(optional)
200g smoked haddock
fillets
1 tbsp crème fraıche
black pepper
a handful of parsley
to serve

DIRECTIONS

1. Slice and wash the leek. Melt the butter in a saucepan and cook the leek gently for 5 minutes until soft but not coloured.
2. Wash and slice the potatoes (there is no need to peel them) and add to the pan with the leek. Cook for 1–2 minutes.
3. Add 150ml of the milk and the vegetable stock. Season well with black pepper and add the chilli flakes, if using. Simmer gently with the lid on for about 15 minutes until the potatoes are cooked.
4. Meanwhile, place the fish in another pan with the remaining milk and poach gently for 5–8 minutes until cooked.
5. Remove the fish from the milk and flake into bite-sized pieces. Pour the poaching liquid into the pan with the vegetables. Stir in the crème fraıche and the flaked fish.
6. Serve in bowls with the chopped parsley.

RHUBARB COBBLER

In my opinion, every veggie plot or garden needs a rhubarb plant.

Each spring, without fuss or complaint, the rhubarb pushes its bright pink buds through the brown earth and slowly unfurls huge umbrella-like leaves on the end of its slender stalks. As a plant, it is both strikingly architectural and delicious.

On our allotment, the arrival of the first stems of tender green rhubarb flushed with softest pink marks the start of our fruit harvest, to be followed not long afterwards by gooseberries and blackcurrants, then, at the height of summer, strawberries, and later on by basketfuls of the sweetest plums.

More often than not, arriving home with an armful of rhubarb, I chop it into chunks and bake in a hot oven with sugar to taste, adding a teaspoon of vanilla paste and a tablespoon or so of water.

Spoonfuls of rhubarb served with yoghurt makes the prettiest of breakfasts, the pink juices mingling with the snowy-white yoghurt, maybe with a sprinkle of nuts and seeds for added crunch. All the better if the nuts have first been lightly toasted in a pan with a little butter and a drizzle of honey or maple syrup.

But to ring the changes, here's a recipe that uses this sometimes underrated fruit.

INGREDIENTS

Serves 4

400g rhubarb,
trimmed and washed

85g caster sugar

1 tsp vanilla paste

150g self raising flour

75g butter

4 tbsp plain yoghurt

1–2 tbsp milk

a handful of flaked almonds

DIRECTIONS

1. Preheat the oven to 180°C fan/350°F
2. Chop the prepared rhubarb into chunks. Place in an ovenproof baking dish with 50g of the caster sugar, the vanilla paste and 2–3 tablespoons of water.
3. Measure the flour into a mixing bowl and rub in the butter to make fine 'breadcrumbs'. Stir in the remaining 35g of caster sugar.
4. Add the yoghurt and enough milk to make a very soft, spoonable dough.
5. Place spoonfuls of the dough onto the rhubarb. There will be gaps, so don't worry if the dough doesn't cover the rhubarb completely. Sprinkle with the flaked almonds.
6. Bake for 30–35 minutes until the topping is golden and the rhubarb tender.
7. Serve with cream, ice-cream or custard.

WILD GARLIC PESTO

Wild garlic is the nervous forager's dream – nothing, except perhaps the familiar blackberry, is so easy to identify.

Growing in damp woodland, the fresh garlic smell is often what first alerts the passer-by to its presence. To be doubly sure, pick a leaf and crush it in your hand to release the unmistakable garlic aroma.

The end of March and beginning of April is wild garlic season. Swathes of glossy green leaves carpet the ground beneath the trees, and collecting a small basketful is one of my favourite things to do at this time of year. Later in the season, the plants are covered in pretty star-shaped white flowers, also edible, but by the time the flowers appear the leaves have lost their bright fresh taste, and soon afterwards the plant dies back.

Wild garlic is particularly versatile. It can be eaten raw or lightly cooked, stirred into soups and risottos or tossed through a salad of mixed leaves. It also makes a great addition to a frittata and an excellent pesto.

It is food for free at its most delicious.

INGREDIENTS

Makes enough to fill one small jar

50g pine nuts

50g Parmesan

75g wild garlic

5–6 tbsp olive oil

juice of 1 lemon

salt

DIRECTIONS

1. Lightly toast the pine nuts in a dry frying pan until golden. Keep an eye on them as they can burn very easily.
2. Grate the Parmesan.
3. Wash the wild garlic and shake to get rid of most of the moisture.
4. Place the pine nuts, wild garlic and Parmesan into a food processor. Blitz until the nuts are roughly chopped, then, with the motor still running, gradually add the olive oil – you may not need all of it. Stop when you have a rough consistency.
5. Scoop the pesto into a bowl and season to taste with the lemon juice and salt, then spoon into a sterilised jar. The pesto will keep in the fridge for a few days.
6. Serve stirred through pasta, added to salad dressings, or to liven up a sandwich.

WILD GARLIC FRITTATA

This frittata makes a lovely lunch or supper dish. If wild garlic is not available, it is equally delicious made with fresh young spinach leaves.

INGREDIENTS

FRITTATA

Serves 4-6

250g small waxy potatoes
½ tbsp oil
a knob of butter
5 spring onions
a small handful of wild garlic or spinach leaves
6 large eggs
salt and pepper
fresh rocket leaves to serve

TOMATO SALAD

20 small cherry tomatoes
juice of half a lime
1 tsp capers
1 tbsp olive oil
a handful of fresh coriander, chopped
salt and pepper

DIRECTIONS

1. You will need a 24cm ovenproof frying pan with a lid.
2. Wash and thinly slice the potatoes. There is no need to peel them.
3. Heat the oil and butter in the frying pan and add the potatoes. Cover with a lid and cook over a moderate heat for 10–15 minutes until golden and tender.
4. Meanwhile, slice the spring onions and wash the wild garlic or spinach.
5. When the potatoes are cooked, add the spring onions and wild garlic or spinach. Cook for 1–2 minutes.
6. In a bowl, beat the eggs and season with salt and pepper.

Pour the eggs into the pan and cook gently until the bottom has set.

7. Preheat the grill to medium and place the pan under the heat to cook for a few minutes until the top is just set. Take care not to overcook.
8. Meanwhile, cut the tomatoes in half. Place in a bowl with the rest of the salad ingredients and season with salt and pepper.
9. Serve the frittata cut into wedges, with the tomato salad and rocket.

PINWHEEL SCONES

I first made these little scones one cold and grey morning when I wanted something to go with a mid-morning cuppa. The scone dough is spread with a buttery, fruity mix then rolled and cut into swirls and finished with lemon icing.

INGREDIENTS

SCONES

Makes 8 scones

200g self raising flour
1 tsp baking powder
50g butter
10g caster sugar
125ml milk

FILLING

40g nuts – pistachios or hazelnuts are good
100g sultanas
50g softened butter
40g caster sugar
1 rounded tsp cinnamon

ICING

50g icing sugar
juice of half a lemon

DIRECTIONS

1. Preheat the oven to 220°C fan/425°F.
2. Butter an 18cm round shallow cake tin.
3. Sift the flour and baking powder into a bowl. Rub in the butter to form 'breadcrumbs' and then stir in the caster sugar.
4. Add enough milk (you may not need it all) and bring the flour mixture together to make a soft dough. Put to one side.
5. Chop the nuts and the sultanas finely to make a rough paste.
6. Roll out the scone dough on a floured surface to form a rectangle approximately 22cm x 30cm.
7. Spread the softened butter over the surface, then sprinkle with the sugar and the cinnamon, followed by the fruit and nut mix.
8. Roll up carefully from a long edge, like a Swiss roll. Cut into 8 equal pieces and arrange in the buttered tin with 7 pieces around the edge and one piece in the middle (see the picture on the left to envisage the arrangement).
9. Bake in the preheated oven for 15–20 minutes until golden.
10. Turn out onto a cooling rack.
11. Make the icing by sieving the icing sugar into a bowl and adding enough lemon juice to make a pourable consistency. When the scones are cool, drizzle with the icing.

LABNEH

Radishes are the sprinters of the veggie plot – a few short weeks after being sown and they are ready to harvest. This makes them particularly appealing to the impatient gardener and very useful for filling in gaps between slower growing crops.

For the past few years, I have grown a variety called Sparkler, a name which seems to perfectly describe this diminutive veggie with its bright pink colour, crunchy texture and peppery taste.

They make a very welcome addition to a leafy salad and also pair well, I think, with something creamy, like this labneh.

INGREDIENTS

Serves 4

2 cups of yoghurt – Greek yoghurt, with its higher fat content, is best here

½ tsp salt

olive oil – a garlic-flavoured oil is good

black pepper

other flavourings, such as thyme leaves, dukkah or chilli flakes

You will also need a piece of muslin and a nylon sieve.

DIRECTIONS

1. Scald the muslin in boiling water, wring out the excess water and use it to line the sieve. Place the sieve over a bowl large enough so that the sieve does not touch the bottom.
2. Mix the yoghurt with the salt and spoon into the lined sieve. Cover lightly and place in the fridge, preferably overnight.
3. The next morning, discard the liquid which has collected in the bowl and spoon the labneh into a serving dish.
4. Drizzle with oil and sprinkle with black pepper and any extra flavourings.

QUICK FLATBREADS

INGREDIENTS

Makes 4

1 cup self raising flour
½ cup yoghurt
¼ tsp salt

DIRECTIONS

1. Mix all the ingredients together to make a smooth dough.
2. Divide into 4 pieces and roll each one out on a floured board to make a rough oval shape.
3. Place on a preheated baking tray in a very hot oven (210°C fan/415°F) and bake for 10–12 minutes, flipping over once whilst baking. Alternatively, cook on a very hot griddle pan for a couple of minutes on each side until browned and cooked through.

CHOCOLATE BUNDT CAKE

In spring, the weather can be unpredictable. April might bless us with beautiful warm sunshine, or torrential rain, or even sleet and snow, and sometimes all three in the space of a few days!

But when it comes to Easter traditions and food, there is no debate: hot cross buns, Simnel cakes, Easter egg hunts… and chocolate. There has to be chocolate.

For this recipe you will need a 1 litre bundt tin.

INGREDIENTS

CAKE

120g plain flour
50g ground almonds
1½ tsp baking powder
120g butter
150g caster sugar
½ tsp almond essence
2 eggs
2 tbsp milk
2 tbsp cocoa powder mixed with 2 tbsp hot water to make a paste
70g dark chocolate chips

ICING

2 tbsp soft butter
55g plain chocolate
115g icing sugar

TO DECORATE

mini chocolate eggs
chocolate shavings (to make chocolate shavings, hold a sharp knife at an angle of 45 degrees on a block of chocolate and drag it towards you)

DIRECTIONS

1. Preheat the oven to 160°C fan/320°F.
2. Butter the bundt tin generously and dust with flour. Put to one side.
3. Mix together the flour, ground almonds and baking powder.
4. Then, in a separate bowl, cream the butter and sugar until light and fluffy. Add the almond essence.
5. Whisk the eggs together and gradually beat them into the creamed mixture, adding a spoonful of the flour and almonds if it looks like the mixture might split.
6. When the eggs are added, fold in the remaining flour and almonds, followed by the milk, the cocoa paste and the chocolate chips.
7. Spoon the batter into the prepared tin and bake for 40–50 minutes until well risen and firm to the touch, and a skewer inserted into the cake comes out clean.
8. Allow the cake to cool in the tin for 10 minutes before turning out onto a wire rack.
9. Meanwhile, make the icing.
10. Put the butter and chocolate into a small pan and heat very gently until the chocolate has melted. Sift in the icing sugar and beat well, gradually adding small amounts of hot water until you have a pouring consistency.
11. When the cake is completely cold, drizzle the icing over and decorate with the chocolate eggs and chocolate shavings.

CINNAMON AND RAISIN LOAF

This is a delicious loaf to serve toasted over the Easter weekend.

It's best to start this recipe first thing in the morning, and though it might seem very complicated at first glance, it is in fact quite straightforward and most of the time the dough is simply resting/rising. And, besides, the smell of freshly baked bread filling the house means it is well worth the effort.

INGREDIENTS

500g strong white bread flour
7g sachet of easy blend yeast
250g raisins
300ml milk
50g butter

50g soft brown sugar
1 egg, beaten
2 tsp cinnamon
½ tsp mixed spice
1 tsp salt

DIRECTIONS

1. Put 200g of the flour, the yeast and the raisins into a large bowl.
2. Warm the milk to 'blood heat' and stir into the flour and yeast mixture.
3. Cover the bowl with a cloth and leave in a warm place for 1½–2 hours until it forms a bubbly batter.
4. Rub the butter into the remaining flour until evenly mixed. Stir in the sugar, cinnamon, mixed spice and salt and add to the bubbly batter with the beaten egg.
5. Mix quickly to make a rough dough. It doesn't matter if it looks lumpy at this stage.
6. Cover the bowl again and leave to rise, in a warm place, for a further hour.
7. After this time, tip the dough onto a lightly floured surface and gently knead for about 10 minutes until you have a smooth ball of dough. It will be sticky to begin with, but resist the temptation to add extra flour.
8. Place the dough back into the bowl, cover and leave for another hour until risen by 50%.
9. Gently remove from the bowl and shape into a round loaf.
10. Place in a floured banneton if you have one, or alternatively on a sheet of baking parchment. Cover lightly and leave for a further hour.
11. When the time is up, preheat the oven to 220°C fan/425°F.
12. If the dough is in a banneton, tip it out onto a sheet of baking parchment. Score the top of the dough in a criss-cross pattern with a sharp knife and lift the dough on the baking parchment onto a large baking tray.
13. Bake in the oven for 20 minutes, then reduce the temperature to 180°C fan/350°F. Continue baking for a further 20 minutes until golden.
14. Leave to cool on a wire rack.

The hedgerow alongside the allotment is awash with cow parsley. Over the past few weeks, what was a tangle of bare brown branches has now become a green and verdant jungle, and as if to welcome the spring sunshine, the frothy white flower heads of the cow parsley sway in the breeze, performing their own version of a May Day dance.

I am enchanted to discover that a family of blue tits has taken up residence in the nest box on the adjoining plot. The chirruping of the baby birds provides a musical backing track as I weed and hoe. Meanwhile, the parent birds keep a wary eye on me from a nearby bush and, when my back is turned, dart into the nest with a tasty morsel for their babies.

Although there is much work going on the allotment, there is little to harvest from the plot at the moment. This is the 'hungry gap', the lull between the end of the autumn /winter crops and the start of the new season. But the month of May marks the beginning of the asparagus season, a vegetable which I have to admit I have never grown but whose arrival in the shops I eagerly await each year.

ASPARAGUS AND RICOTTA TART

INGREDIENTS

Serves 4–6

1 sheet of ready-rolled puff pastry
10–12 spears of asparagus
1–2 tbsp olive oil
60g Parmesan
250g ricotta
1 lemon
whole nutmeg for grating
a few sprigs of thyme
fresh rocket leaves
a handful of pine kernels (optional)
salt and pepper

DRESSING

juice of 1 lemon (see above)
3–4 tbsp olive oil
salt and pepper

DIRECTIONS

1. Preheat the oven to 200°C fan/375°F.
2. Unroll the pastry, keeping it on the baking parchment which it comes with. Lightly score 1.5cm from the edge along all four sides. Place on a baking tray.
3. Wash and trim the asparagus, drizzle with the olive oil and season with salt and pepper. Place on a baking tray in a single layer.
4. Put the asparagus on the top shelf of the oven and the pastry underneath. Cook the asparagus for 10–12 minutes until tender and the pastry for 15–18 minutes until golden and cooked through.
5. Meanwhile, shave off a few curls of Parmesan with a potato peeler and reserve for decoration. Grate the remainder.
6. Mix together the ricotta, the Parmesan, the zest of the lemon, a good grating of fresh nutmeg and a few leaves from the thyme. Season well with salt and pepper.
7. Pat down the middle of the cooked pastry case with the back of a spoon and spread with the ricotta mixture. Top with the asparagus and the remaining thyme leaves. Return to the oven for 5–8 minutes.
8. Make a dressing with the juice of the lemon, 3–4 tablespoons of olive oil, and salt and pepper.
9. Drizzle the dressing over the tart and scatter the pine kernels over, if using. Sprinkle the cooked tart with the Parmesan curls. Serve with rocket leaves.

Eventually it's time to plant out the bean seedlings. It's a day that always fills me with slight trepidation. For several weeks, I have nurtured the little plants on the kitchen windowsill, watching as the first shoots appear and the tiny new leaves unfurl, tenderly watering them until, tall and straight with several sets of leaves each, they are ready to face the big wide world on the allotment.

I plant them carefully in neat rows, each with a tall cane to support them, wondering how they would fare on their own and hoping they won't be buffeted by wind and rain (the weather in May can be very unpredictable) or prove an irresistible snack for passing slugs and snails.

A couple of days later, I'm back at the allotment to check on things and am relieved to see the little seedlings looking fine and seeming settled in their new home. With a bit of luck, they will soon be twisting their way up the canes and on their way to producing a tasty harvest!

By this time, the spinach sown a few weeks ago is also growing well, with the first flush of baby leaves. In a few weeks, there should be enough to enjoy in a leafy mixed salad or perhaps to make the following recipe.

SPINACH PANCAKES WITH SMOKED SALMON

INGREDIENTS

PANCAKES

Makes 12–15 pancakes. Any not needed for this recipe can be frozen, interleaved with baking parchment.

180g plain flour
300ml milk
1 egg
75g baby spinach, washed
pinch of salt
oil for frying

FILLING

150g hot smoked salmon
200ml crème fraiche
juice of half a lemon, plus extra lemon wedges for serving.
½ tbsp capers – chopped
½ tbsp chopped dill
a little chopped red chilli
black pepper

TO SERVE

green salad

DIRECTIONS

1. Prepare the filling. Flake the salmon and set aside. Mix the crème fraiche together with the other filling ingredients and season with black pepper.
2. Place all the ingredients for the pancakes, except the oil, into a blender and whizz to a smooth batter.
3. Heat a drizzle of oil in a small frying pan.
4. When hot, add a large spoonful batter and quickly swirl around to cover the base of the pan. Cook on a moderate heat, on one side only, until golden underneath.
5. Move the pancake to a plate and keep warm whilst cooking the rest of the batter.
6. Spoon a little of the crème fraiche filling mixture onto each pancake and add some of the flaked salmon. Serve with a green salad. Any extra crème fraiche can be served separately.

POLENTA CAKE WITH VANILLA POACHED RHUBARB

INGREDIENTS

Serves 6-8

175g soft butter
175g caster sugar
3 eggs
130g polenta
45g ground almonds
1 tsp baking powder
20g flaked almonds
½ tsp vanilla paste

POACHED RHUBARB

5–6 stalks of rhubarb
caster sugar to taste
½ tsp vanilla paste

TO SERVE

extra flaked almonds (optional)
icing sugar for dusting
cream or crème fraiche

DIRECTIONS

1. Butter and line a 20cm springform cake tin with baking parchment.
2. Preheat the oven to 170°C fan/340°F.
3. In a large bowl, cream the butter and sugar together until light and fluffy.
4. Beat the eggs in a small bowl and stir in the vanilla paste.
5. In another bowl, mix together the polenta, ground almonds and baking powder.
6. Gradually beat the eggs into the creamed mixture, adding a spoonful of the dry ingredients if the mixture looks like it might split.
7. When all of the eggs are incorporated, gently fold in the rest of the dry ingredients.
8. Spoon the mixture into the prepared tin and sprinkle with the flaked almonds.
9. Bake in the centre of the oven for 40–50 minutes until firm to the touch.
10. When baked, leave to cool in the tin for 10 minutes, then turn out onto a cooling rack.
11. Meanwhile, trim and chop the rhubarb into chunks. Place in a shallow lidded pan, add sugar to taste, the vanilla paste and a splash of water.
12. Put the lid on and cook gently for 10 minutes or so until the rhubarb is tender but still holds its shape.
13. Sprinkle the cooled cake with the extra flaked almonds if using and dust with icing sugar. Serve with the poached rhubarb and a dollop of cream or crème fraiche.

Summer

Summer. The strawberries are beginning to ripen, turning slowly from green, through pink to luscious red, but it seems we are not the only ones to find them irresistible; birds, slugs, snails, woodlice and even ants all seem to want to partake in the feast. Since we are trying to garden organically on the allotment, chemical sprays are not admissible, so slowly I am learning to accept the less than perfect – the leaf where the edge has been nibbled, the strawberry with a small hole in it – learning that 'supermarket perfect' is not a necessity. And besides, nothing beats the flavour of a home-grown strawberry, plucked from the plant and eaten there and then whilst sitting on the steps of the shed, even if it does have a tiny hole in it!

This is a simple sponge cake, flavoured with finely chopped pistachios and sandwiched together with a luscious strawberry and rosewater filling.

Rosewater is a beautifully perfumed flavouring, and one which I most associate with a favourite Christmas treat – Turkish delight. I can well understand Edmund (from *The Lion, The Witch and The Wardrobe*) being seduced into betraying his friends for some. There is something so irresistible about the prettily decorated wooden boxes, the sweet icing sugar that wafts up as the box is opened, and the delicate, perfumed taste of the pastel-coloured squares.

STRAWBERRY SPONGE CAKE WITH VANILLA, PISTACHIO AND ROSEWATER

INGREDIENTS

SPONGE CAKE

175g softened butter
175g caster sugar
175g self raising flour
1 tsp baking powder
3 eggs
½ tsp vanilla paste
55g pistachios

STRAWBERRY FILLING

200g strawberries, plus extra for decoration
1–2 tbsp caster sugar
½ tsp rosewater

MASCARPONE FILLING

200g mascarpone
1 tbsp icing sugar, sieved
½ tsp vanilla paste
½ tsp rosewater

DIRECTIONS

1. Butter and line 2 x 19cm sandwich tins.
2. Preheat the oven to 170°C fan/340°F.
3. Mix all the cake ingredients together, except the pistachios, and beat for 1–2 minutes.
4. Finely chop or grind the pistachios, then gently fold them into the mixture.
5. Divide the mixture evenly between the two tins.
6. Bake for 20–25 minutes until well risen and golden.
7. Allow to cool in the tins and then turn out onto a cooling rack.
8. Meanwhile, make the strawberry filling. Wash the strawberries and put into a small pan with 1 tablespoon of water and the sugar. Cook gently for about 10 minutes until the strawberries have just collapsed.
9. Remove the strawberries with a slotted spoon and place in a dish.
10. Boil the remaining juice for 1–2 minutes or until it coats the back of a spoon. Allow to cool, then stir in the rosewater.
11. Mix the mascarpone with the icing sugar, then stir in the vanilla paste and rosewater.
12. When ready to serve, place the bottom layer of the cake onto a serving plate. Liberally spread with the mascarpone and top with the strawberry filling. Carefully place the second sponge on top and decorate with the remaining strawberries and a dusting of icing sugar.

PEA AND LETTUCE SOUP WITH CHIVES AND BASIL

I have had mixed results growing peas, and one particular year they were a disaster. I bought small seedlings from the local nursery and planted them with great anticipation, only to find a few days later that they had been munched by slugs, until just a short stump remained. So I conceded defeat, cut my losses and decided a pack of frozen peas would have to suffice.

This is a delicious, quick and light summer soup.

INGREDIENTS

Serves 3-4

4–5 spring onions
1 clove garlic
1 litre chicken or vegetable stock
500g peas, fresh or frozen
1 lettuce – about 300g (I used Little Gem)
1 lemon
olive oil for frying
salt and pepper

TO SERVE

a few tablespoons single cream
fresh basil and chives
lemon zest
a handful of microgreens

DIRECTIONS

1. Chop the spring onions and crush the garlic.
2. Heat a small amount of oil in a pan, add the spring onions and garlic and sauté for 4 minutes until soft.
3. Add the stock, peas and chopped lettuce and cook gently for about 5 minutes until the lettuce has wilted
4. Purée the mixture in a blender and season to taste with salt and pepper.
5. Garnish with the cream, chopped basil, chives, a sprinkle of lemon zest and the microgreens.

QUICK PEA AND PRAWN PASTA

Late evening on the allotment and the hedge is alive with birds. Their song fills the air – a beautiful evensong in this outdoor cathedral.

I sit for a moment on the wooden chair next to the shed. Above, the sky is a uniform silver grey, and overhead swifts soar lazily, whilst a hungry blackbird hops around the veg plot searching for tasty morsels. The air is very still, with barely the whisper of a breeze. There is the deep-throated coo of a wood pigeon in a nearby tree, and in the distance the sound of muffled voices.

I water a few seedlings and sow another row of Swiss chard and beetroot.

Rain is forecast for tomorrow, though in this, one of the driest areas of the country, it rarely amounts to much.

On evenings like this, a light supper seems perfect. This goes nicely with a glass of white wine.

INGREDIENTS

Serves 2

1 clove garlic
½ red chilli
1 tbsp oil
½ tsp red Thai curry paste
400ml chicken stock
200ml tinned coconut milk
2 nests of egg noodles
200g frozen jumbo king prawns – defrosted
2 handfuls of frozen peas
juice of half a lemon
chopped parsley to garnish

DIRECTIONS

1. Chop the garlic, then de-seed and chop the chilli.
2. Heat the oil in a large pan, add the garlic, chilli and Thai curry paste and fry for 1–2 minutes.
3. Add the chicken stock and coconut milk and bring to the boil.
4. Add the noodles, reduce the heat to a simmer and cook for a further 1–2 minutes.
5. Add the prawns, peas, lemon juice and parsley.
6. Heat through until the noodles are tender and the prawns are cooked thoroughly.
7. Serve in deep bowls garnished with parsley.

COCONUT AND LIME PANNA COTTA

Coconut and lime are the tastes of summer, and this is a simple, light and delicious dessert that can be made ahead of time and which makes a wonderful ending to a meal.

INGREDIENTS

PANNA COTTA

Serves 6

5 leaves gelatine
400ml tin of coconut milk
2 tbsp caster sugar
½ tsp vanilla paste
zest of 1 lime (save the juice for the lime syrup)
400ml single or double cream

LIME SYRUP

3 limes
2 cups granulated sugar

TO SERVE

dried edible rose leaves
toasted desiccated coconut

DIRECTIONS

1. Soak the gelatine leaves in a bowl of cold water for 10 minutes until soft.
2. Meanwhile, heat the coconut milk and sugar in a pan until just simmering and the sugar has dissolved.
3. Remove from the heat and stir in the vanilla paste and the lime zest.
4. Drain the gelatine leaves and add to the coconut milk mixture. Stir until the leaves have dissolved.
5. Leave to cool slightly, then stir in the cream.
6. Pour into 6 ramekins or pretty tea cups and place in the fridge for several hours until set.
7. While the panna cotta are chilling, prepare the lime syrup and lime slices.
8. Squeeze the juice from the leftover lime used for the panna cotta and take the zest and juice from one other lime. (To maximise the juice, heat the limes in the microwave for 20 seconds each.)
9. Add water to make the juice and zest up to 300ml and pour into a small pan.
10. Add the granulated sugar and heat gently until the sugar dissolves.
11. Slice the remaining 2 limes thinly, add to the syrup in the pan and simmer gently for 15–20 minutes.
12. Remove the lime slices and drain on parchment paper.
13. Toast a little desiccated coconut in a small pan for a minute or two, then allow to cool.
14. Serve the panna cotta with the lime syrup and lime slices. Decorate with the rose leaves and toasted coconut.

Any leftover lime syrup will keep in the fridge for a couple of weeks and makes a refreshing drink diluted with still or sparkling water. The remaining lime slices can be left to dry further overnight and then stored in an airtight container and used to decorate other desserts or cakes.

Any lime syrup left over from making coconut and lime panna cotta will keep in the fridge for a couple of weeks and makes a refreshing drink diluted with still or sparkling water.

The sweetcorn are taller than me. They stand proud and straight, like soldiers on parade, their silky tassels, like the plume on the helmets of the Household Cavalry, moving gently in the breeze.

It is one of nature's many miracles that a small, wizened kernel planted at the beginning of the year can, within a few short months, grow to be plant over six foot tall. When the tassels turn a chocolate brown, I know the cobs are ready to be harvested. They are delicious simply grilled, served with butter and maybe a squeeze of lemon juice, or they make a wonderful addition to summer salads such as this one.

GRILLED CORN AND COURGETTE GRAIN SALAD

INGREDIENTS

Serves 2 as a main dish
or 4 as a side dish

120g bulgar wheat (or mixed grains)
2 corn on the cob
1 tbsp olive oil
1 large courgette (zucchini)
1–2 tsp mild sweet smoked paprika
a few dried chilli flakes
2 large handfuls mixed fresh herbs, such as mint, parsley and chives
salt and pepper

DRESSING

4 tbsp olive oil
1½ tsp chipotle paste
juice of 1–2 lemons
salt and pepper

TO SERVE

1 lemon, grilled (optional)
feta or goat's cheese

DIRECTIONS

1. Cook the bulgar wheat in lots of boiling, salted water according to the instructions on the packet, then drain. Tip into a large bowl.
2. Meanwhile, make the dressing by whisking together the olive oil, chipotle paste and the juice of one lemon. Season with salt and pepper to taste.
3. Pour half the dressing over the drained bulgar wheat and leave to cool.
4. Preheat the grill or a griddle pan to medium. Brush the corn on the cob with olive oil and season with salt and pepper. Grill, turning from time to time, until tender and lightly charred.
5. When cooked, rub with the smoked paprika and carefully slice the corn kernels off the cob. Keep to one side.
6. Slice the courgette. Heat a little oil in a frying pan and add the courgette in one layer if possible. Season with 1 teaspoon of salt and cook over a medium heat until tender and browned in places.
7. Remove from the heat and add a squeeze of lemon juice.

ASSEMBLE THE SALAD

8. If using the lemon, cut in half and place cut side down in the pan in which the courgettes were cooked. Turn the heat to high and sear the cut lemon until browned.
9. Mix the courgettes, corn and chopped fresh herbs into the bulgar wheat. Sprinkle with a few chilli flakes and extra smoked paprika. Top with crumbled feta or goat's cheese.
10. Serve the remaining dressing separately.

OVEN-ROASTED TOMATOES

Growing your own tomatoes is one of summer's little pleasures.

A home-grown, sun-ripened tomato is a world away from the often insipid imported ones found in supermarkets. My favourites are the little cherry tomatoes.

Delicious picked and eaten straight away for lunch, this recipe is useful at the end of the season, when the tomatoes are particularly abundant and need to be preserved in some way.

They make a delicious addition to all manner of dishes.

INGREDIENTS

1kg cherry tomatoes

4 tbsp garlic-infused olive oil (or ordinary olive oil, if this is not available)

2 tsp salt

2 tsp sugar (optional)

1 tbsp chopped rosemary

a large pinch dried chilli flakes

DIRECTIONS

1. Preheat the oven to 120°C fan/250°F.
2. Cut the tomatoes in half around the middle. Place cut side up, in one layer, on a large baking tray. Drizzle with the olive oil and sprinkle over the other ingredients.
3. Roast in the oven for 3–4 hours until shrivelled and starting to brown around the edges.
4. When cool, store in an airtight container in the fridge.

oven roasted tomatoes

FENLAND LOTTIE

Along with the little plum tree, the blackcurrant bush was one of the first things to be planted on our allotment. Every year it has produced an abundant harvest of glossy, black berries, and the pungent woodsy smell of the leaves as I rummage amongst the branches to gather the clusters of fruit always reminds my of the garden in my childhood home. It was a long garden, much bigger than the average garden these days, and the far end (about a third in total) was reserved for fruit and veg. Here, Mum and Dad grew a range of vegetables, but what I mostly remember are the fruit bushes – gooseberry, blackcurrant and, my favourite as a child, the raspberry canes which, come summer, were weighed down with delicious ruby-red berries.

These days, I still love raspberries, but I have also come to appreciate the sharper taste of blackcurrants. They make the most delicious jam, the inherent acidity balancing the sugar, and the leaves, if steeped in boiling water for a few minutes, make a refreshing drink served with lemon and a teaspoon of honey.

I also love them in these crumble bars, but if you can't find fresh blackcurrants in the shops (they seem very difficult to source, most of the commercial harvest going, I suspect, to make a well-known fruit squash), a bag of frozen mixed berries is a perfect alternative.

BLACKCURRANT CRUMBLE BARS

INGREDIENTS

Makes 10-12 squares

THE BASE

280g self raising flour
30g ground almonds
55g icing sugar
175g softened butter
1 tbsp milk

FRUIT TOPPING

350g blackcurrants, stalks and ends trimmed.
125g caster sugar
2 tbsp cornflour
4 tbsp flaked almonds

If blackcurrants are not available, use 350g mixed frozen berries but reduce the caster sugar to 80–100g according to taste

DIRECTIONS

1. Grease and line a 19cm x 28cm shallow baking tray with baking parchment.
2. Preheat the oven to 180°C fan/350°F.
3. Mix the flour, ground almonds and icing sugar in a bowl. Rub in the softened butter to make 'breadcrumbs', then stir in the milk to bring the mixture roughly together.
4. Press two thirds of the mixture into the tin and smooth out with the back of a spoon.
5. Chill in the fridge whilst you prepare the fruit.
6. Mix the blackcurrants (or frozen fruit), caster sugar and cornflour with 1 tablespoon of water and bring to the boil in a pan.
7. Bubble for 3–4 minutes, then remove from the heat and allow to cool slightly.
8. Spoon the fruit mixture over the crumble base, sprinkle over the rest of the crumble mix and scatter over the flaked almonds.
9. Bake in the preheated oven for about 30 minutes until golden.
10. Allow to cool in the tin and then cut into squares.

COURGETTE FRITTERS

Everyone who has an allotment or veggie plot and has grown courgettes (or zucchini if you're over the pond!) can tell you tales of courgette gluts. At the beginning of the year, it is very tempting to plant several plants, maybe different-coloured varieties, but be warned – by the end of August they will have taken over your life!

A single plant, once established, can produce countless fruit almost, it would seem, overnight, and any hidden under leaves and overlooked will turn into giant marrows whilst your back is turned! But don't let this put you off. Courgettes are delicious and endlessly versatile: they can be eaten raw, grilled or roasted, stirred into a mixed grain salad, grated into cake batter where they make a delicious light and fragrant bake, or made into little fritters and served with a crisp green salad for lunch.

INGREDIENTS

Makes about 10 fritters

350g courgettes, grated weight (approximately 2 large courgettes)
90g self raising flour
80ml milk
2 eggs
¾ tsp salt
¼ tsp mild smoked paprika
15g chopped parsley
2 tbsp chopped chives
25g Parmesan, grated
pinch chilli flakes
oil for shallow frying

FOR THE YOGHURT SAUCE

4 tbsp yoghurt
a couple of tablespoons mixed, chopped fresh herbs, such as parsley and mint
salt and pepper
a little olive oil (1–2 tsp)
2 tsp mango chutney (optional)

DIRECTIONS

1. Place the grated courgettes in a clean tea towel and squeeze out as much liquid as possible.

2. Tip into a bowl and stir in the remaining ingredients.

3. Heat a small amount of oil in a frying pan over a medium heat. Drop spoonfuls of the mixture into the pan and fry until golden on one side.

4. Flip the fritters over with a spatula and fry for a minute or two on the other side.

5. Remove and keep warm whilst frying the remaining mixture.

6. Mix the ingredients for the sauce together.

7. Serve the fritters with the yoghurt sauce, a green salad and, if wished, some cooked grains on the side.

There are some simple activities that seem to encapsulate slow summer days, and shelling peas and beans in a quiet shady part of the garden is one of those.

There is nothing better than the sweet taste of a freshly podded pea or the soft feel of the inside of a fur-lined broad bean pod.

This recipe makes the most of these delicious summer vegetables.

If you have the time, double podding the beans by blanching them in boiling water for a couple of minutes and then removing the pale outer skin to reveal the emerald beans inside is well worth the extra effort.

RICOTTA DUMPLINGS WITH BASIL PESTO

INGREDIENTS

DUMPLINGS

Makes about 20 dumplings

250g ricotta
50g Parmesan
75g plain flour plus extra for dusting
zest of half a lemon
¼ red chilli, finely chopped
salt and pepper
2 egg yolks, beaten

PESTO

30g pine nuts plus extra for serving
30g Parmesan, grated
a handful of fresh basil
100ml olive oil
juice of half a lemon
salt and pepper

TO SERVE

150g peas, fresh or frozen
150g broad beans, fresh or frozen
a handful of fresh mint
a handful of fresh chives

DIRECTIONS

1. Tip the ricotta into sieve, set over a bowl and leave to drain for 1–2 hours.
2. Meanwhile, make the pesto.
3. Toast the pine nuts in a pan over a medium heat until golden. Leave to cool, then place in a food processor with the grated Parmesan and the basil.
4. Blend briefly, then gradually add the oil to form a sauce. Taste, and season with salt and pepper and the lemon juice. Put to one side while you continue with the dumplings.
5. When the ricotta has finished draining, tip away any liquid that has collected in the bowl.
6. Mix together the drained ricotta, grated Parmesan, plain flour, lemon zest, chopped chilli, and salt and pepper. Stir in the beaten egg yolks. Do not overwork the mixture or the dumplings will be tough.
7. Using two teaspoons, form the mixture into small balls roughly the size of a conker and drop onto a floured tray. The mixture should make about 20 dumplings.
8. At this point, the dumplings can be chilled in the fridge if required.
9. When ready to serve, bring a large pan of salted water to the boil, reduce to a simmer and, using a slotted spoon, carefully lower a few of the dumplings into the water.
10. Cook until they float to the top, about 4–5 minutes.
11. Remove them with the slotted spoon and drain on kitchen paper while you cook the rest of the dumplings.
12. Meanwhile, lightly cook the peas and beans in another pan of boiling water.
13. When all the dumplings are cooked, serve in large bowls with the basil pesto, the peas and beans, the chopped mint and chives and a few extra pine nuts.

RASPBERRY FRIANDS

In my mind, raspberries rival strawberries for the 'top summer berry' spot.

Just a few of these luscious fruits can transform a breakfast pancake, a bowl of yoghurt or a cake.

For several years we grew autumn fruiting raspberry canes on the allotment, but discovered they were somewhat unruly and had a habit of sending out runners which popped up in unexpected places, such as the middle of the pumpkin patch. My raspberry growing experience was revolutionised when I realised that raspberry bushes suitable for growing in pots were available – and I haven't looked back since!

These little cakes, known as 'friands', are popular in Australia and New Zealand, and rightly so. They are light and moist and perfect with a cuppa.

Friands are traditionally oval in shape, but if you don't have a friand cake mould then a muffin pan will work just as well.

INGREDIENTS

Makes 6 friands

80g butter, melted
35g plain flour
75g ground almonds
100g icing sugar
3 egg whites
a small punnet of raspberries
extra butter for greasing the tin

DIRECTIONS

1. Grease a six-hole friand or muffin tin with butter.
2. Preheat the oven to 180°C fan/350°F.
3. Mix the flour, ground almonds and icing sugar in a bowl.
4. Lightly whisk the egg whites until foamy and slowly stir into the dry ingredients.
5. Carefully mix in the melted butter.
6. Spoon the mixture into the baking tin, dividing equally between the holes, and top each cake with two raspberries.
7. Bake in the oven for 18–20 minutes until golden.
8. Leave to cool in the tin then place on a cooling rack.
9. Any leftover raspberries can be blended, sweetened to taste with honey, and served as a sauce.

EASY PEACH TRIFLES WITH CARDAMOM

When temperatures soar, climbing steadily towards 30°C, visits to the allotment are consigned to the margins of the day – to very early morning or late in the evening, when temperatures are a little more bearable.

At such times, watering takes precedence over other tasks. Courgettes, squash and beans, to name but a few, are thirsty plants and, like me, are craving a long, cool drink of water. So I dip the can into the dark depths of the rain barrel and pull out bucketfuls of water to pour onto the grateful plants.

This is not so much a recipe, more a list of ingredients to assemble. But it's perfect for a summer's day and a good way to use those peaches which simply refuse to ripen properly.

INGREDIENTS

Serves 4

4 peaches
4 cardamom pods
2 tbsp maple syrup or honey
8 almond cantuccini/biscotti
200ml Greek yoghurt
200ml ready-made vanilla custard
1 tbsp icing sugar

TO FINISH

a few handfuls of flaked almonds
a little extra maple syrup or honey

DIRECTIONS

1. Preheat the oven to 200°C fan/400°F.
2. Wash the peaches, cut them in half and remove the stones.
3. Place in a single layer on a small baking tray, drizzle over the maple syrup or honey and add 4–6 tablespoon of water.
4. Remove the cardamom seeds from the pods and grind finely in a pestle and mortar. Sprinkle the ground seeds over the peach halves.
5. Bake in the oven for 20–30 minutes until the peaches are tender, adding a little more water if they are starting to catch on the bottom of the tray.
6. Meanwhile, break the cantuccini into chunks and mix the icing sugar into the Greek yoghurt.
7. When the peaches are ready, reserve three halves and purée the rest in a blender.
8. Divide the peach purée between four small serving glasses. Layer up with the cantuccini, yoghurt and custard, dividing equally between the glasses.
9. Slice the reserved peach halves and use to top the trifles. Add the flaked almonds and an extra drizzle of maple syrup or honey.
10. Chill in the fridge for a few hours before serving.

Years ago, in my early twenties, I stopped one late summer afternoon at a roadside stall and bought several pounds of beautiful ripe plums. I had no garden to speak of then, and certainly no allotment, so those plums were like treasure to me. I took them home, found a recipe in an old book and made my first batch of jam. I still remember the thrill and sense of satisfaction at seeing a neat row of jars lined up with their jewel-like contents.

Since then, I have made countless jars of jam and chutney, but the thrill and sense of satisfaction has never diminished. There is an alchemy to preserving, a magical transmutation that occurs when fruit and/or veggies meet sugar and spices. Nothing beats opening a jar of homemade jam in the middle of winter, dolloping spoonfuls onto warm toast and remembering summer's bounty.

PLUM JAM

This recipe is from *River Cottage Handbook No. 2: Preserves* by Pam Corbin, a book I really recommend for anyone wanting to delve deeper into the wonderful world of preserving.

INGREDIENTS

1.5 kg plums
1.25 kg granulated sugar

YOU WILL NEED

a very large saucepan or preserving pan
about 8 medium-sized jars and lids which have been sterilised *
a long-handled wooden spoon
a large ladle and a funnel are also useful

*To sterilise jars and lids, either put them through the hot cycle of a dishwasher or hand wash in hot soapy water, dry with a clean cloth and place in an oven heated to 150°C fan/300°F for 20 minutes.

DIRECTIONS

1. Before you begin, place several small saucers into the freezer. These will be used later to test for setting point.
2. Halve and stone the plums, then place in the pan with 400ml water. Simmer gently for about 20 minutes until the plums are tender and the skins are soft.
3. With the pan still on a gentle heat, add the sugar and stir until it is dissolved. It is important that the sugar has fully dissolved, so I check this by stirring the mixture with a wooden spoon and examining the back of the spoon for any undissolved sugar crystals.
4. When the sugar has fully dissolved, turn the heat up to a fast rolling boil and boil for 10 minutes.
5. At this point, turn off the heat and spoon a little of the jam onto one of the saucers from the freezer. Wait for a minute or two, then check for a set by pushing the mixture with your finger. If it wrinkles, then the jam is set. If not, continue boiling and check again at 3-minute intervals.
6. When the jam has set, allow it to cool a little, then carefully ladle it into the jars, filling right to the top. Screw the lids on, and label the jars when cold.

Autumn

Autumn arrives with a chill in the morning, mist hovering across the river, and a heavy dew on the grass. An extra layer in the form of a thick jumper is needed on my early morning trips to the allotment.

As I push open the gate, my eye wanders over our little plot. The lush green of summer is being replaced by shades of brown and ochre. The climbing beans, their leaves now crumpled and brown and the few remaining pods wrinkled and wizened, whisper 'winter is coming' as the wind catches them. The sound of leaves rustling in the breeze is the music of early autumn.

But on the far side of the plot, still attached to their roots by long twisting tendrils, lie the bright orange orbs of the Hokkaido squash. These small pumpkins are one of my favourites, easy to grow and delicious to eat. I will be collecting my beautiful golden harvest today and taking them home. They will be stored in a cool, dry shed and be the basis of many meals right up until Christmas.

SQUASH AND LENTIL PASTA BAKE

INGREDIENTS

Serves 4

250g squash (prepared weight). I used Hokkaido, but butternut squash would be good too

1 medium onion

1 clove garlic, crushed

200g mushrooms

2 tsp mild smoked paprika

1 x 400g tin tomatoes

200ml vegetable stock

1 x 250g pack cooked puy lentils

1 tsp soy sauce

1 tbsp balsamic vinegar

3 tbsp crème fraiche

5 sheets fresh lasagne

35g grated Parmesan

olive oil

salt and pepper

DIRECTIONS

1. Preheat the oven to 200°C fan/400°F.

2. Peel and chop the squash into bite-sized pieces. Season with salt and pepper and drizzle with 1 tablespoon of olive oil. Toss to coat and spread in a single layer on a baking sheet.

3. Roast for 20–30 minutes until tender. Remove from the oven and reduce the temperature to 180°C fan/350°F.

4. Meanwhile, peel and chop the onion. Heat another tablespoon of oil in a pan, add the onion and crushed garlic and sauté for 5–10 minutes until soft. Remove to a plate.

5. Add a little more oil to the pan and fry the chopped mushrooms over a fairly high heat until golden.

6. Return the onion to the pan and add the smoked paprika. Stir, then add the tinned tomatoes, the stock and the lentils.

7. Simmer for 15 to 20 minutes until thickened. Season well with salt and pepper and add the soy sauce and balsamic vinegar.

8. Stir in the roasted squash and the crème fraiche then spoon into an ovenproof dish.

9. Tear the lasagne into rough pieces and poke into the lentil mixture. Leave some pieces to stick out, as these go crispy. Sprinkle with the Parmesan and bake for 20–30 minutes until golden and bubbling.

10. Serve with a green salad.

MINESTRONE SOUP WITH CRISPY KALE

The pretty pink, speckled borlotti bean is easy to grow and a welcome addition to the allotment.

Unlike green beans, it is not a bean to be eaten whole. Early autumn is the time to harvest them, when the pods are turning brown and the autumn winds blow, rattling the beans inside their cases. Gather the pods and remove the beans, drying them for use at a later date. They will keep for many months in a sealed container.

INGREDIENTS

Serves 4

100g fresh borlotti beans
3 cloves garlic (1 whole, 2 chopped)
1 medium onion, chopped
1 medium carrot, chopped
1 stick celery, chopped
1 litre vegetable stock
2 tbsp tomato purée
1 tbsp red tomato pesto
70g small pasta, such as orzo
30–50g Parmesan, grated
2 big handfuls kale
a little olive oil
salt and pepper

DIRECTIONS

1. Tip the borlotti beans into a saucepan, cover with water and add 1 whole clove of garlic peeled. Bring to the boil and boil for 5 minutes, then simmer for another 20–30 minutes until the beans are tender.

2. Add 1 teaspoon of salt and leave the beans to cool in the water, then drain.

3. Meanwhile, heat a little oil in a large saucepan and add the onion, carrot and celery, the remaining 2 cloves of garlic, chopped, and a pinch of salt. Cover and cook over a medium heat for about 10 minutes until the vegetables are soft.

4. Add the stock, the tomato purée and red tomato pesto, and the pasta. Bring to a boil and then reduce the heat and simmer for 15–20 minutes until the pasta is cooked.

5. Finally, add the previously cooked beans and heat through.

6. While the soup is cooking, preheat the oven to 180°C/350°F.

7. Roughly chop the kale, sprinkle with a little salt and a drizzle of olive oil and massage the ingredients together until the kale is covered. Spread on a baking tray and cook in the oven for about 10 minutes until crispy.

8. To serve, ladle the soup into bowls and top with a generous handful of grated Parmesan and some of the crispy kale.

GROWING BEETROOT

Growing up, beetroot was only available from the shops in large jars, sliced and pickled in mouth-puckering vinegar, to be served alongside a few lettuce leaves and cucumber slices, the beetroot juices turning everything an unappetising pink colour. Consequently, early on, I decided that beetroot wasn't for me.

Then came the advent of veg boxes, delivered to the door and bursting with fresh seasonal vegetables, and in particular, bunches of beautiful beetroot – naked, so to speak, except for their deep purple stalks and ruby-veined leaves. And I discovered that beetroot are delicious roasted and served with goat's cheese, grated and eaten raw in salads with carrot, apple and red cabbage, made into warming soups and, maybe best of all, mixed with dark chocolate to make the most delectable cakes.

So when we got our allotment, beetroot was one of the first vegetables that I sowed, a reliable variety called Bolthardy. I marvelled at the way the tiny seeds grew into beautiful carmine-coloured roots and the fact that the leaves also made a delicious salad ingredient akin to spinach.

And now, beetroot is a mainstay on the veg plot, and one of our favourites.

ROASTED BEETROOT SOUP WITH HORSERADISH CREAM AND HERBY DUMPLINGS

INGREDIENTS

Serves 2

3–4 medium beetroot, approximately 500g unpeeled weight
1 medium carrot
1 medium red onion
1–2 tbsp olive oil
½ tsp cumin seeds
salt and pepper
1 litre vegetable stock
1 rounded tsp tomato purée
1 tbsp red wine vinegar

DUMPLINGS

Makes about 10

75g self raising flour
¼ tsp salt
35g butter
2 tbsp finely chopped mixed herbs
(I used dill, chives and parsley)

TO SERVE

2–3 tbsp creamed horseradish
2–3 tbsp plain yoghurt

DIRECTIONS

1. Preheat the oven to 200°C fan/400°F.
2. Peel and chop the vegetables into small pieces and place on a baking tray in a single layer. Drizzle with the oil, season with salt and pepper and sprinkle with the cumin seeds.
3. Roast for about 30 minutes until golden and tender.
4. Meanwhile make the dumplings. Mix the flour and salt together and rub in the butter to make a mixture resembling breadcrumbs.
5. Stir in the herbs and add 1–2 tablespoon of water to make a dough.
6. Pinch off pieces of dough and roll into balls about the size of a walnut. You should get about 10 balls.
7. Place on a baking tray and bake in the oven along with the vegetables for about 15 minutes until the dumplings are cooked through.
8. When the vegetables are cooked, tip into a saucepan and add about 700ml of the vegetable stock, reserving the rest.
9. Stir in the tomato purée and vinegar, heat through and then blend, adding the reserved stock if it seems too thick.
10. To serve, mix the horseradish cream and yoghurt together. Spoon the soup into deep bowls, add a little horseradish cream and a few dumplings.

Who doesn't enjoy rooting through the hedgerows on a warm September's day, basket in hand, looking for blackberries? Maybe it's the idea of food for free or the hunter-gatherer instinct buried deep in our DNA which makes this pastime so inherently satisfying. Even a few scratches can't diminish the pleasure, and whether you live in an urban environment or the middle of the countryside, there is bound to be a patch of land nearby where the hardy bramble has made its home.

And, in addition, nature in her providence ensures that blackberries ripen just at the same time as the English apple season arrives, making possible a favourite flavour combination – blackberry and apple.

BLACKBERRY AND APPLE GALETTE

The joy of a galette lies in its rustic, free-form appearance. All the deliciousness of a pie but without the stress!

INGREDIENTS

Serves 6-8

340g plain flour
170g butter
55g icing sugar
1 egg yolk
3 tbsp milk

1 extra tbsp milk for glazing
150g blackberries plus extra to serve
1 tbsp caster sugar
2 red-skinned eating apples
2 tbsp apricot jam
1–2 tbsp chopped hazelnuts for garnish (optional)

DIRECTIONS

1. Place a large baking sheet in the oven and preheat the oven to 190°C fan/375°F.
2. In a large bowl, rub the butter into the flour until the mixture resembles breadcrumbs.
3. Stir in the icing sugar.
4. Whisk the egg yolk and 3 tablespoons of milk together in a small jug and stir into the flour mixture, bringing it together with your hands to make a dough. Cover the dough loosely and rest in the fridge whilst you prepare the fruit.
5. Tip the blackberries into a pan, then add the caster sugar and 1 tablespoon of water. Bubble for about 5 minutes until you have a loose jam-like consistency. Allow to cool.
6. Roll out the pastry on a large piece of baking parchment to form a rough circle about 32cm diameter. No need to be precise here.
7. Spread the cooled blackberry purée over the pastry, leaving a 4cm border around the edge.
8. Thinly slice the apples and arrange in overlapping circles on top of the blackberries. Fold the pastry border in and brush with the tablespoon of milk. Sprinkle with the chopped hazelnuts if using.
9. Using the baking parchment to help, carefully lift the galette and paper onto the hot baking sheet and bake for 30–35 minutes until golden.
10. Leave to cool slightly on a cooling rack.
11. Meanwhile, heat the apricot jam in a small pan with the same quantity of water and bubble for a minute or two to make a thin syrup. Use this to brush over the warm galette as a glaze.
12. Serve with extra blackberries and cream or ice-cream.

AUBERGINE AND WHITE BEAN STEW

I always think the aubergine (or eggplant to our American readers!) is a very beautiful vegetable. In the greengrocers, it sits proudly amongst the rows of more homely produce. The unpretentious potato, turnip, swede or sprout cannot compete with the aubergine's handsome, glossy, purple skin.

As befits such a regal vegetable which hails from climates much warmer than our own, it requires heat and sun to grow well and so really needs the protection of a greenhouse to thrive in the unpredictable British summer. It is not a vegetable I have ever tried growing, but it is one of my favourites to cook with.

This recipe is my adaptation of a delicious dish I had one time in a restaurant. I love the sweet and sour combination of flavours.

INGREDIENTS

Serves 4

2 medium aubergines

1 red onion

2 cloves garlic, chopped

pinch chilli flakes

1 tsp dried oregano

2 tbsp capers in brine, drained and rinsed

4 tbsp pitted black olives

3 tbsp balsamic vinegar, plus extra for serving

a small can (227g) of tomatoes

400g can cannellini beans

2 handfuls raisins

1 tbsp tomato purée

2 tbsp olive oil, plus extra for serving

salt and pepper

fresh mint or parsley to serve

DIRECTIONS

1. Chop the aubergine into bite-sized chunks. Slice the onion.
2. Heat the oil in a pan and add the aubergine. Cook over a high heat for 5 minutes or so until golden.
3. Lower the heat (adding a little more oil if necessary) and add the onion and a pinch of salt. Cover and cook until the onion is soft and translucent – about 5 minutes.
4. Add the chopped garlic, chilli flakes, oregano, capers, olives and vinegar. Cook for a minute or two, then add the tinned tomatoes, the drained beans and the raisins
5. Pour in 100ml hot water and the tomato purée and simmer gently for about 15 minutes.
6. Season well with salt and pepper. Add a little more hot water, if necessary. I like a fairly soupy consistency.
7. Spoon into deep bowls to serve, add extra vinegar to taste and a drizzle of olive oil.
8. Scatter over the chopped mint or parsley and serve with crusty bread.

There can be few things nicer than the unexpected gift of a basket of fruit from a neighbour's or friend's garden left on the doorstep. And so it was that I found myself with several pounds of pears, straight from a friend's pear tree, organic and with zero food miles!

Apart from eating them just as they are – a ripe pear is a delectable thing – I decided to bake a few in the oven, sprinkled with ground ginger and drizzled with maple syrup. They make a lovely addition to morning porridge or, served with a chunk of homemade gingerbread cake, a delicious pudding.

Ginger cake always seems to me to be the perfect autumn/winter cake. Maybe it's all those wonderful spices, so evocative of the festive season to come.

SPICED GINGERBREAD

INGREDIENTS

Makes 10-12 squares

225g self raising flour
2 tsp ground ginger
½ tsp ground cinnamon
½ tsp bicarbonate of soda

100g butter
225g soft brown sugar
2 tbsp black treacle
1 egg
4 tbsp milk
50g crystallised stem ginger

DIRECTIONS

1. Line a 19cm x 28cm shallow baking tin with parchment paper.
2. Preheat the oven to 170°C fan/340°F.
3. Sieve the flour, spices and bicarbonate of soda into a large bowl.
4. Place the butter, sugar and black treacle into a small pan and heat gently until melted.
5. Allow to cool slightly.
6. Whisk the egg and milk together and chop the ginger into small pieces.
7. Pour the cooled, melted butter mixture onto the dry ingredients, followed by the egg and milk and the ginger pieces. Stir until just combined, then spoon into the prepared tin.
8. Bake for about 30 minutes until risen and firm to the touch.
9. Cool on a wire rack and cut into squares before serving.

BAKED PEARS

INGREDIENTS

Serves 4 on their own, or 8 as an accompaniment to the gingerbread

4 pears
½ tsp ground ginger
2 tbsp maple syrup

Ice cream and a few chopped nuts (optional) to serve.

DIRECTIONS

1. Cut the pears in half through the stem. No need to peel.
2. Place in a baking dish. Sprinkle with the ground ginger and drizzle over the maple syrup.
3. Depending on the ripeness of the pears, bake for 20–30 minutes until tender.
4. Serve with ice cream and a few chopped nuts.

MUSHROOM AND SQUASH RISOTTO WITH THYME

The evenings are closing in; each day the curtains drawn a little earlier. Flip-flops are replaced with slippers, and a jumper pulled from the back of the cupboard adds an extra layer of warmth. In a few weeks, the clocks will change and we will be heading towards winter proper.

This is the time for comfort food – root vegetables made into robust and warming soups, beans and lentils transformed into hearty stews, rice and pasta dishes bursting with veggie goodness. I have grown butternut and Hokkaido squash successfully on the allotment, and both are very good in this recipe, but butternut squash are easier to find in the shops.

A mixture of wild mushrooms looks pretty, but button mushrooms are just as tasty in this dish.

INGREDIENTS

Serves 4

450g squash, peeled, deseeded and cut into bite-sized pieces

1 tsp mild smoked paprika

about 350g mixed mushrooms

1 medium onion, finely chopped

1 small stick celery, finely chopped

300g risotto rice

1 litre chicken or vegetable stock

1 lemon

olive oil

a knob of butter

a small bunch thyme

salt and pepper

DIRECTIONS

1. Toss the squash with a drizzle of olive oil, the smoked paprika and a seasoning of salt and pepper and roast in an oven preheated to 200°C fan/400°F for 20–25 minutes until soft and golden.

2. Meanwhile, cut any large mushrooms in half. Heat a knob of butter in a large pan and fry the mushrooms with a few sprigs of thyme until golden. Remove to a plate.

3. Add another small knob of butter to the pan and fry the onions and celery for 5–10 minutes until golden.

4. Tip the rice into the pan and cook for a minute or two.

5. Heat the stock to simmering point in another pan and add a ladleful at a time to the rice mixture, stirring all the time until the rice has absorbed the stock. Continue gradually adding the stock and stirring until all the stock is used and the rice is tender.

6. Add a squeeze of lemon juice to the roasted squash, then add the squash to the risotto mixture along with the mushrooms.

7. Cook for a further minute until everything is piping hot. Serve straight away.

SPICED PUMPKIN MUFFINS

Pumpkin makes a delicious addition to cakes in much the same way as carrot or beetroot does.

These muffins, with a choice of two fillings, make a lovely breakfast or teatime treat.

INGREDIENTS

Makes 12

200g (deseeded and peeled weight)
275g self raising flour
1 tsp baking powder
2 tsp cinnamon
1 tsp mixed spice
125g soft brown sugar
100g butter
180ml milk
2 large eggs
50g chopped walnuts

FILLING

12 tsp marmalade
or 120g cream cheese
1 tbsp caster sugar
zest of 1 orange

DIRECTIONS

1. Preheat the oven to 180°C fan/350°F.
2. Line a twelve-hole muffin tin with muffin cases.
3. If using the cream cheese filling, mix the cream cheese, sugar and orange zest together and put to one side.
4. Chop the squash and whizz to a fine purée in a food processor.
5. Sift the flour, baking powder and spices into a large bowl. Stir in the sugar.
6. Melt the butter in a small pan and allow to cool.
7. In a separate bowl, whisk the eggs, milk and cooled butter together.
8. Add the wet ingredients to the dry ingredients along with the puréed squash and stir gently with a metal spoon until just combined. Take care not to overmix the ingredients. It doesn't matter if there are a few lumps.
9. Half fill the muffin cases with the cake batter, add 1 teaspoon of your chosen filling, then top up with the remaining muffin mix.
10. Sprinkle with the chopped walnuts and bake in the preheated oven for 20–25 minutes until well-risen and golden.
11. Cool on a wire rack.

APPLE, SULTANA AND PECAN LOAF

Some of the nicest picnics we have enjoyed as a family have been those in early autumn. No swatting away of annoying flies or belligerent wasps intent on getting to your food before you've had a chance to open the picnic basket, and no fear of heat rash or sun burn or overheated sandwiches – or, worse, overheated children. Instead, a little warm sun (if you're lucky) augmented by woolly jumpers and scarves, maybe a flask of hot soup to sip from a mug and a slice of delicious homemade cake.

This apple, sultana and pecan loaf fits the bill perfectly, being easily transportable and especially scrumptious when spread thickly with butter.

INGREDIENTS

225g self raising flour
110g butter
110g brown sugar
1 rounded tsp cinnamon
1 rounded tsp mixed spice
2 medium-sized eating apples
230g sultanas
2 eggs
1–2 tbsp milk
50g pecans, chopped

DIRECTIONS

1. Preheat the oven to 180°C fan/350°F.
2. Line a 900g loaf tin with baking parchment.
3. In a large bowl, rub the butter into the flour. Stir in the sugar and spices.
4. Grate the apples (no need to peel) and add to the mixture along with the sultanas.
5. Whisk the eggs and 1 tablespoon of milk together and stir into the other ingredients, adding a further 1 tablespoon of milk if necessary to make a soft, spoonable mixture.
6. Spoon into the prepared tin and sprinkle with the chopped pecans.
7. Bake for 50 minutes to 1 hour, or until a skewer inserted in the middle comes out clean. Cover the cake with foil towards the end of cooking if it is browning too much.
8. Leave to cool in the tin for 10 minutes and then remove and finish cooling on a rack.
9. Serve spread generously with butter.

ROASTED HAZELNUT, CHOCOLATE AND PLUM TRAY BAKE

For me, the humble plum is one of my favourite stone fruits. Unlike imported peaches and nectarines, which never seem to ripen properly, a home-grown, sun-ripened plum, with its deep ruby-coloured skin freckled with gold, and sweet amber flesh, is a late summer treat.

The plum tree on our allotment was one of the first things Rob, aka Mr Digandweed, and I planted, an unnamed variety rescued from the 'bargain basement' corner of the local garden centre.

Each year in spring, it delights with a cloud of frothy white blossom, and then, in late summer, huge basketfuls of sweet ripe plums. With such an abundance, I can usually be found stirring a big pan of bubbling fruit and sugar, ready to be potted up into jars and stored in the cupboard. A jar of plum jam taken down from the shelf on a cold winter's day, spoonfuls to be spread thickly on hot buttered toast, is very welcome reminder of a far-off summer.

But if a small punnet of plums is all that's available, this cake is a delicious way to enjoy them.

INGREDIENTS

Makes 12 squares

125g soft butter
125g soft brown sugar
125g self raising flour
1 tsp baking powder
2 large eggs
100g ground roasted hazelnuts
125g dark or milk chocolate (or a mixture of the two), melted
6 plums
4 tbsp chopped hazelnuts
2 tbsp plum jam to glaze

DIRECTIONS

1. Preheat the oven to 180°C fan/350°F.
2. Line a shallow 28cm x 19cm baking tin with parchment paper.
3. In a large bowl, whisk the butter, sugar, flour, baking powder and eggs together, then stir in the hazelnuts and chocolate.
4. Spoon the mixture into the prepared tin.
5. Halve the plums, remove the stones and place on top of the cake batter. Sprinkle with the chopped hazelnuts and bake in the preheated oven for 30–35 minutes until well risen and golden.
6. Warm the plum jam in a small pan and sieve to remove any lumps.
7. When the cake is cooked, leave to cool in the baking tin for 10 minutes then remove to a cooling rack. Brush the cake with the warm jam to glaze.

RED ONION AND WINDFALL APPLE CHUTNEY

Onions are probably one of the easiest vegetables to grow and one of the most utilised in the kitchen. This recipe uses red onions from the allotment and windfall apples from my daughter's garden. Fills three medium-sized jars.

INGREDIENTS

1kg red onions
500g cooking apples
2 fat cloves garlic
5cm piece root ginger
¼ tsp dried chilli flakes
1½ tsp salt
50g raisins
250g brown sugar
500ml red wine vinegar

DIRECTIONS

1. Roughly chop the onions. Peel, core and roughly chop the apples. Peel and chop the garlic and ginger into small pieces.
2. Place all the ingredients into a very large, wide, stainless steel pan and bring to the boil, stirring from time to time.
3. Reduce the heat and let the chutney simmer for 2½ to 3 hours until you have a jam-like consistency. Stir occasionally towards the end of the cooking time to ensure the chutney does not burn on the bottom of the pan.
4. The chutney is ready when a wooden spoon drawn across the base of the pan leaves a channel which doesn't fill immediately with vinegar.
5. While the chutney is cooking, wash several jars and vinegar-proof lids (i.e. ones with a plastic lining – most jars of jam now have these) in very hot water. Dry with a clean cloth and put into an oven heated to 150°C fan/300°F for about 15 minutes.
6. Turn the oven off but leave the jars inside until you are ready to fill them.
7. When the chutney is cooked, ladle into the jars, seal with the lids, and label when cold.
8. Chutney is often better if left to mature for about a month until opening.

red onion and windfall
apple chutney

FENLAND LOTTIE

Winter

CELERY SOUP WITH CHORIZO

The deep, rich, fertile soil of the Fens is particularly suited to the cultivation of Fenland celery, a heritage crop which dates back to Victorian times. Fenland celery has a short season of just 8–10 weeks from October to December and was grown in the Fens to be transported to markets in London, where it was a very popular addition to the Victorian Christmas dinner table. But, over the years, it slowly fell from popularity, until recently, when local farmers revived this delicious vegetable, and once again consumers can enjoy its sweet, nutty flavour.

The practice of growing it in wide deep trenches and 'earthing it up' with black soil as it grows contributes to its distinctive pale colour. It is then harvested by hand, when the root is cut into a point. During the later months of the year, I can often find Fenland celery for sale in local shops, the black earth still clinging to it. It's then that I like to make this delicious, creamy soup.

INGREDIENTS

Serves 4

30g butter
1 medium onion, chopped
1 head celery (about 500g), chopped
1 large potato (about 450g), chopped
1 litre vegetable stock
150ml single or double cream
2–3 tbsp olive oil
100g chorizo sausage (optional)
a couple of slices of crusty bread for croutons

DIRECTIONS

1. Melt the butter in a large pan. Add the chopped onion, celery and potato and sauté gently with the lid on for about 5 minutes.
2. Add the vegetable stock and simmer for a further 20–25 minutes until the potatoes are tender.
3. Blitz in a blender, season to taste with salt and pepper, stir in the cream and reheat gently.
4. Meanwhile, make the croutons. Roughly tear the bread into bite-sized chunks, drizzle with olive oil and bake in a preheated oven at 180°C fan/350°F for 10–15 minutes until crisp and golden.
5. If using the chorizo, heat 1 teaspoon of oil in a pan, chop the chorizo into small pieces and fry until golden, about 10 minutes.
6. Serve the soup in deep bowls with, the croutons and chorizo sprinkled on top.

CHEESE AND LEEK SCONES

Who doesn't love a freshly baked scone!

Plain scones, crisp on the outside yet fluffy within, served with lashings of clotted cream and jam, or fruited scones enriched with plump raisins or fragrant with orange zest and cardamom, all to be enjoyed with a pot of tea.

Alternatively, a savoury scone can be delicious, flavoured with herbs or spices, black olives, sun-dried tomatoes, bacon – the possibilities are endless!

Or, as here, with cheese and leeks added, perfect with a bowl of soup on a cold winter's day, or with extra cheese and some homemade chutney as a light lunch.

Quick and easy, scones were one of the first things I learnt to bake as a child.

My most favourite are those made with buttermilk, which seems to give extra lightness and fluffiness to the baked scone.

INGREDIENTS

Makes 8 scones

2 leeks
225g self raising flour
(all white flour or, as I used here, half white and half wholemeal)
75g butter, plus extra for frying
2–3 tablespoons buttermilk
1 large egg
¼ tsp mustard
75g cheese, grated
salt and pepper

DIRECTIONS

1. Preheat the oven to 220°C fan/425°F.

2. Wash and finely chop the leeks. Melt a small knob of butter in a pan and cook the leeks gently for about 8 minutes until soft. Allow to cool.

3. Put the flour into a large bowl and season with salt and black pepper. Rub the butter into the flour until it resembles breadcrumbs. Stir in the grated cheese (keep back a couple of spoonfuls for topping later) and the cooled leeks.

4. Mix 2 tablespoons of buttermilk with the egg and mustard and add to the mixture in the bowl. Bring the ingredients together to form a soft dough. Do not overwork the dough.

5. As soon as it forms a ball, put it on a floured surface and roll out to no less than 2.5 cm thick. This is one of the secrets to well-risen scones, so don't be tempted to roll too thinly.

6. Cut into rounds and place on a greased baking sheet. Brush the tops with the remaining buttermilk and sprinkle over the reserved cheese.

7. Bake for 10–12 minutes until well risen and golden.

8. Cool on a wire rack.

9. Best enjoyed on the same day.

WINTER ROOT VEGETABLE SALAD

Celeriac is one of those vegetables often bypassed on the shop shelves – an 'ugly duckling' of a vegetable, resembling a knobbly and somewhat misshapen swede.

I first came across celeriac as a child on holiday with my parents in France, when, in the form of celeriac remoulade, it made an appearance in almost every French deli. Grated and mixed with creamy mustardy mayonnaise, it was one of my favourite things to eat on our impromptu picnics as we toured around the country.

I have tried growing celeriac on the allotment, without, I have to admit, much success, the resulting roots being tiny and even more knobbly than usual. But it still remains one of my favourite winter vegetables and with its delicious nutty flavour makes a lovely winter salad.

INGREDIENTS

Serves 2-3

½ medium celeriac
3 medium carrots
1 red-skinned eating apple

FOR THE DRESSING

2 limes
4 tbsp olive oil
small, thumb-sized piece of root ginger
a pinch of chilli flakes
a large handful of fresh coriander
a large handful of roasted peanuts
salt and pepper

DIRECTIONS

1. Grate the celeriac, carrots and apple and place in a bowl.
2. Whisk the ingredients for the dressing together and pour over the vegetable mixture.
3. To serve, scatter with the chopped coriander and chopped peanuts.
4. If you are wondering what to do with the remaining celeriac, it makes a delicious mash with equal quantities of potato.

SMOKEY BEANS WITH CHORIZO

As the days get colder and the nights get longer, bonfire night comes as a welcome distraction.

Much as I love the huge, awe-inspiring public firework displays, there is something quite special about standing around a bonfire with family and friends, a sparkler held in gloved hand.

And, of course, there has to be food – warming, comforting food.

Jacket potatoes seem to be the perfect choice here: crisp on the outside, fluffy within, with a delicious filling.

INGREDIENTS

Makes enough to fill 4 jacket potatoes

75g chorizo, chopped
1 small onion
1 stick celery
1 clove garlic
1 heaped tbsp mild, smoked paprika
1–2 tbsp olive oil
2 tsp chipotle paste
500g passata
1 tsp vegetable stock powder
1 tbsp soft brown sugar
2 x 400g tins cannellini beans
salt and pepper

TOPPING

1 avocado
1 small red onion
juice of 1 lime

TO SERVE

large handful parsley, chopped
soured cream

DIRECTIONS

1. Start with making the topping. Peel the avocado, remove the stone, and chop into small pieces.
2. Peel and thinly slice the red onion.
3. Put the avocado and onion into a bowl with the lime juice and season with salt and pepper.
4. Leave to marinate whilst you prepare the beans.
5. Heat the oil in a large pan and fry the chopped chorizo for a minute or two.
6. Using a slotted spoon, remove the chorizo to a plate, leaving the flavoured oil behind.
7. Chop the onion and celery and add to the pan with the minced garlic. Add a pinch of salt, then cover and cook slowly until the onion is soft and translucent.
8. Add the smoked paprika and chipotle paste and cook for a minute.
9. Return the chorizo to the pan and stir in the passata, stock powder, sugar and both tins of drained beans.
10. Season with salt and pepper and simmer, uncovered, for about 30 minutes, adding a little water if it seems a bit dry.
11. Use to fill the jacket potatoes, topping with the avocado and onion, the soured cream and chopped parsley.

ROASTED CAULIFLOWER GRATIN

November can be grey and wet. But the rain means that the earth is soft and the hoe slides through the soil, like a knife through butter, as I do a bit of late season weeding on the allotment. There are overwintering onions to plant, probably slightly late if truth be told, but they must be planted now if they are to stand any chance of sending out roots before winter proper starts.

The rest of the plot is looking a little bare; just a few beetroot and Swiss chard leaves remain. But I like these early winter days on plot 84b and the sense of solitude and peace as winter descends.

Cold and wet November weather requires a warming supper, and this recipe is my adaptation of an old favourite, cauliflower cheese. Instead of steaming the cauliflower in the usual way, I roast it in the oven with red onion and spices, which I think intensifies the taste and gives a lovely nutty flavour to the finished dish.

INGREDIENTS

Serves 3-4 as a main meal

1 medium cauliflower
1 medium red onion
1 tsp cumin seeds
1 tsp mild smoked paprika
3–4 tbsp olive oil
salt and pepper
50g butter
50g plain flour
600ml semi skimmed milk
100g mature cheddar cheese
3–4 tbsp grated Parmesan

DIRECTIONS

1. Preheat the oven to 190°C fan/375°F.
2. Break the cauliflower into florets and peel and chop the onion into wedges. Toss the vegetables with the cumin, paprika, salt and pepper, and the oil. Spread in one layer onto a shallow baking sheet and roast in the oven for 20–30 minutes until tender and golden.
3. Meanwhile, melt the butter in a pan and stir in the flour. Cook for a minute or two over a medium heat, then gradually add the milk, little by little, stirring well after each addition to make a smooth sauce.
4. Cook again over a low heat for 2–3 minutes, stirring all the while, then remove from the heat.
5. Add the cheddar cheese and season with salt and pepper.
6. Preheat the grill.
7. Spoon the roasted vegetables into a shallow ovenproof dish, pour the sauce over and sprinkle the Parmesan on top
8. Grill until bubbling and golden.

RAISIN AND HAZELNUT OAT COOKIES

Inevitably, we get to the first snow of the winter. At first, soft flakes begin to fall, landing gently, silently, on the bare branches of shrubs and trees in the garden, their touch feather light. At first, it seems the plants barely notice the snow's caress, but as more snow falls, they began to bow under the weight, arching gracefully towards the ground. Eventually the garden is transformed into a wonderland of white, until an imperceptible rise in temperature means snow turns to sleet, and sleet to rain, and the magic is gone.

These are days to stay at home, to be cosy in the kitchen, to bake.

These cookies are perfect for making on a cold winter's day and are delicious enjoyed whilst sipping hot chocolate, snuggled under a blanket with a good book.

INGREDIENTS

Makes 12 large cookies

115g soft butter
110g soft brown sugar
1 large egg, beaten
½ tsp vanilla extract
2 tbsp maple syrup
95g wholemeal plain flour
1 tsp baking powder
1 tsp cinnamon
pinch of salt
120g rolled oats
100g raisins, or 50g raisins and 50g dried cranberries
20g pumpkin seeds
20g chopped hazelnuts

DIRECTIONS

1. Cream the butter and sugar together in a large bowl.
2. Gradually beat in the egg, vanilla extract and maple syrup.
3. Mix the flour, baking powder, cinnamon and salt together, then stir into the creamed mixture. Add all the other ingredients and mix to form a stiff dough.
4. Scoop up balls of dough (an ice-cream scoop is useful here), place on a greased baking sheet and flatten slightly with a fork.
5. Chill in the fridge for an hour then bake at 170°C fan/340°F for 12–15 minutes, until just brown around the edges but slightly soft in the middle.
6. Cool on a wire rack and store in an airtight tin.

'JAMMY DODGER' STARS

These biscuits are great to make with children in the run-up to Christmas and can make a lovely last-minute gift.

Makes about 30, depending on the size of the cutters.

You will need 2 star-shaped cutters – one medium and one small.

INGREDIENTS

150g soft butter

100g caster sugar

1 egg, beaten

½ tsp vanilla paste

300g plain flour

jam to sandwich the biscuits together

icing sugar to dust

DIRECTIONS

1. Put the butter and sugar into a bowl and cream together. Add the beaten egg and vanilla paste and mix well.

2. Gradually add the flour, stir well and bring the mixture together to form a ball.

3. Wrap the dough in cling film and chill in the fridge for up to an hour.

4. Remove the dough from the fridge and preheat the oven to 180°C fan/350°F.

5. Roll out the dough on a floured board to about the thickness of a pound coin.

6. Cut out as many stars as possible using the larger cutter, re-rolling the dough as necessary. Then, with the smaller cutter, cut out a star shape from the middle of half of the stars.

7. Place on a greased baking sheet and bake for 10–12 minutes until just golden. The leftover stars from the middle of the biscuits can also be baked and are lovely as tiny biscuits with a cup of coffee.

8. Cool the biscuits on a cooling rack.

9. When completely cold, sandwich the biscuits together with the jam, matching each cut biscuit with an uncut biscuit. A red-coloured jam looks particularly festive.

10. Dust with icing sugar to serve.

HOMEMADE MINCEMEAT

It might seem foolhardy in the run-up to Christmas, when schedules are tight and lists are long, to suggest making homemade mincemeat, especially when jars of the stuff are readily available in the shops. But for me, Christmas is as much about the preparation and baking beforehand as it is the day itself. Those cosy hours spent cooking and baking in the kitchen are entwined with a multitude of memories.

Memories from childhood… of Mum, just before we set off for Midnight Mass on Christmas Eve, hastily spreading royal icing on the Christmas cake and adding the plastic robin and snowman which made an annual appearance. Or the time Mum, Dad, my sister and I arrived in the snow on Christmas Day to visit Grandma in her hilltop home in Wales, and the smell of Grandma's wonderful bread sauce warming on the stove.

Memories as an adult … of Christmas with our first daughter, just a few days old, the best Christmas present ever. Of Christmas with excited toddlers, new toys and wrapping paper spread everywhere. Memories of school nativity plays and the year our second daughter (aged 4) was an oh-so-serious golden-haired angel. Or the year Mr Digandweed dressed up with cotton wool beard and Santa hat and pretended he was the man himself.

These are the thoughts which fill my mind as I mix and stir.

This recipe for mincemeat involves nothing more than a little weighing, chopping and mixing and, if you make it, I hope you will agree that it far surpasses anything that can be bought in the shops. I have been known to creep into the kitchen at night and eat big spoonfuls of it straight from the jar!

INGREDIENTS

4 tbsp coconut oil

250g dark brown sugar

1 cooking apple, peeled, cored and grated.

250g raisins

200g sultanas

150g dried cranberries

50g stem ginger in syrup, finely chopped, plus 2 tbsp syrup

75g glacé cherries, chopped

½ tsp mixed spice

½ tsp freshly grated nutmeg

1 lemon, zest and juice

150ml brandy

DIRECTIONS

1. Gently melt the coconut oil and sugar in a pan.

2. Put all the other ingredients, except the brandy, into a bowl and add the coconut oil mixture. Stir well, then add the brandy.

3. Cover the bowl and leave overnight for the fruit to absorb the brandy.

4. The following day, spoon into very clean jars.

5. Store in the fridge and use to fill individual mince pies or larger tarts.

MINCEMEAT ICE CREAM

If you have any of the mincemeat left over, then this no-churn ice-cream, based on a recipe by Mary Berry, is absolutely delicious.

INGREDIENTS

Serves 6

4 large eggs, separated
100g caster sugar
300ml double cream
150g mincemeat
3 ginger nut biscuits, crumbled (optional)

DIRECTIONS

1. Whisk the egg whites in a large, spotlessly clean bowl until stiff peaks form.
2. Slowly whisk in the sugar a spoonful at a time, and continue whisking until you have a stiff meringue.
3. Whisk the cream in a separate bowl to soft peak stage. Do not over whisk.
4. Gently fold the cream, beaten egg yolks, mincemeat and crumbled biscuits (if using) into the meringue.
5. Pour into a plastic container and freeze for several hours or overnight.

The winter months are peak season for all types of citrus fruit.

I love the diminutive clementines and mandarins, delicious and refreshing over the Christmas period, and when January arrives, I search the shelves for Seville oranges. With their knobbly, unprepossessing appearance, they are not a fruit to be enjoyed raw, but simmered in water and then bubbled with sugar, they are transformed into the most superlative marmalade. Making Seville orange marmalade is one of my favourite January rituals.

But for eating raw and juicing, my favourite is the blood orange, with its freckled skin and flesh rippled with flashes of red. A glass of freshly squeezed ruby-red juice is perfect on a January morning, but they also make a wonderful orange curd, a beautiful preserve with the consistency of softly whipped cream and delicate flavour of sweet oranges.

It's only recently that I have discovered a method for making orange curd in the microwave, which makes this particular recipe very quick and easy.

MICROWAVE ORANGE CURD

INGREDIENTS

Makes enough to fill two small jars

juice and zest of 4–5 oranges, about 200ml in total
150g caster sugar
150g butter, melted
4 egg yolks

DIRECTIONS

1. Sterilise two small jars, either by washing with very hot water and then putting in an oven preheated to 150°C fan/300°F for 15 minutes, or by running through the hot cycle in a dishwasher.
2. Scrub the oranges and remove the zest. If possible, use organic, unwaxed oranges, and although I used blood oranges for this recipe, other oranges make an equally delicious curd.
3. Whisk the sugar and eggs in a microwave-safe bowl until smooth.
4. Whisk in the orange juice and stir in the zest and melted butter.
5. Cook in the microwave on high for 30-second bursts, stirring after each interval, until the mixture coats the back of a spoon.
6. It should take 4–5 minutes in total. The curd will thicken further as it cools.
7. Don't overheat the mixture or be tempted to cook it for longer intervals, otherwise you risk ending up with orange-flavoured scrambled eggs!
8. If the worst happens and there are bits of overcooked egg in your mixture, simply strain through a sieve and no-one will be any the wiser!
9. Pour into the sterilised jars and label when cool.
10. Once opened, store in the fridge and use within 2 weeks.

CHICKPEA AND COCONUT NOODLES

A quick and warming noodle dish for a cold winter's day.

INGREDIENTS

Serves 4

2 medium leeks
1 stick celery
1 tbsp oil
1 clove garlic
1 tsp harissa paste
1 tsp vegetable stock powder
1 x 400g tin chickpeas, drained
1 x 400g tin coconut milk
1 tbsp peanut butter
1 lemon
2 nests egg noodles
100g fresh baby spinach

TO SERVE

roasted peanuts
1 lime

DIRECTIONS

1. Heat the oil in a pan, add the washed, chopped leeks and celery, add a pinch of salt and cook covered, on a moderate heat, for 5–10 minutes until soft.

2. Add the crushed garlic clove and harissa paste, stir for a minute or two, then add the stock powder, 400ml hot water, the drained chickpeas, coconut milk, peanut butter, juice of half a lemon and the noodles. Season with salt and pepper.

3. Cover and cook for about 10 minutes until the noodles are soft.

4. Add the spinach right at the end and cook until it is just wilted.

5. Serve in bowls with lime wedges and a few roasted peanuts.

HOMEMADE GRANOLA

January is a much maligned month, often dismissed as dreary, an anti-climax after the festivities of Christmas and the New Year, a damp squib of a month. But January has its own treasures: a pale, grey light that soothes, the bright green of a daffodil shoot pushing through the brown earth, the sight of the tiniest of buds on a hedgerow branch or the unexpected delight of a sea of bobbing white snowdrops on a roadside verge.

At home, I crave order and simplicity, a decluttering as we enter a new year and all that it promises.

And so I often find myself sorting out the kitchen cupboards at this time of year. If, like me, you find your cupboards are harbouring half-used packets of nuts, dried fruit and seeds – leftovers from Christmas baking – then this homemade granola is a delicious way of using them up.

Serve with milk or yoghurt and fresh fruit for breakfast, or sprinkle over ice cream for dessert.

This recipe makes enough to fill 2 medium-sized jars.

INGREDIENTS

1½ cups of mixed nuts
(use whatever is to hand – I used almonds, hazelnuts and pecans)

4 tbsp coconut oil

4 tbsp maple syrup or runny honey

2½ cups of oats
(or 2 cups of oats and ½ cup of rye flakes)

1 cup of pumpkin seeds

1 cup of sunflower seeds

½ cup of desiccated coconut

2 cups of dried fruit
(again, use whatever is in the cupboard. I used sultanas, raisins and dried cranberries)

3–4 tsp cinnamon

DIRECTIONS

1. Preheat the oven to 180°C fan/350°F.

2. Chop the mixed nuts into small pieces. You can do this in a food processor, but I find the results are more even if chopped by hand.

3. Melt the coconut oil and maple syrup or honey in a pan over a low heat.

4. Meanwhile, put the remaining ingredients, except the dried fruit and cinnamon, into a large bowl. Pour over the melted coconut oil mixture and stir well to coat all the ingredients evenly.

5. Spread in a single layer onto a large baking sheet and bake in the oven for 30–40 minutes, stirring well every 10 minutes, until golden and toasted.

6. Allow to cool, then add the fruit and cinnamon.

7. Store in an airtight jar.

ONE CUP PANCAKES

With Shrove Tuesday on the horizon, my thoughts turn to pancakes, and it's at this time of year that I wonder why I don't make them more often. Quick, easy and versatile, I remember with particular fondness the thin, lacy crêpes that Mum used to make, simply served with a squeeze of lemon juice and a sprinkling of sugar.

These thicker, smaller 'one cup' pancakes are very good too. They make a wonderful brunch, served with grilled bacon and maple syrup, or as here, with a quick blueberry chia jam, a sprinkling of chopped nuts and a drizzle of maple syrup or honey.

INGREDIENTS

Choose a medium-sized cup or mug as a measure. Makes 10-12.

1 cup self raising flour
a pinch of salt
1 cup milk
1 large egg
½ tsp vanilla paste (optional)
a little butter or oil for frying

DIRECTIONS

1. Sift the flour and salt into a mixing bowl, add the egg and milk and whisk together to make a smooth batter.
2. Stir in the vanilla paste, if using.
3. Place a large frying pan over a medium heat and add a knob of butter or a tablespoon of oil. When the butter or oil is hot, drop large spoonfuls of the batter into the pan, allowing room for them to spread a little.
4. Cook for 1–2 minutes until small bubbles appear on the surface and the bases are golden. Flip each pancake over with a fish slice and cook until golden on the underneath.
5. Transfer the pancakes to a plate and keep warm.
6. Repeat with the remaining batter.

BLUEBERRY CHIA JAM

Chia seeds are the edible seeds of a flowering plant from the mint family. They absorb many times their own weight in water and are good as a thickening agent so are useful for making spoonable fruit 'jams' without the need for a lot of refined sugar. Try to use Medjool dates if possible for this recipe as they give a lovely, rich fudge-like taste to the finished jam.

INGREDIENTS

Makes one small jar.

500g blueberries
2 tbsp water
1½ tbsp chia seeds
1 tsp vanilla paste
10 Medjool dates
1–2 tbsp maple syrup

DIRECTIONS

1. Gently cook the blueberries with the water until just soft.
2. Place in a high-speed food blender with the chia seeds, vanilla paste and dates.
3. Blend until smooth and then sweeten to taste with the maple syrup.
4. Spoon into a sterilised jar and store in the fridge for up to a week.